meta • noia

Noun – (me-ta-noi- ə\) :
A transformative change of heart

A little book of essays by
Betsy Chasse

Edited by
Cate Montana and Renee Slade
Artwork and design by Ri Stewart

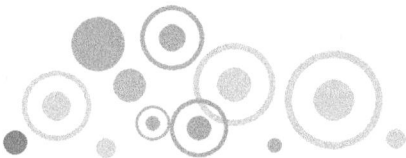

For the me I have been looking for.

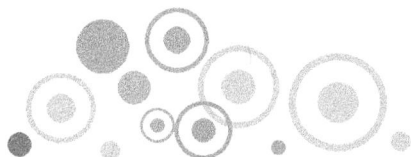

When we get out of the glass bottle of our ego,
and when we escape
like squirrels in the cage of our personality
and get into the forest again,
we shall shiver with cold and fright.
But things will happen to us
so that we don't know ourselves.
Cool, unlying life will rush in,
and passion will make our
bodies taut with power.
We shall laugh, and
institutions will curl up
like burnt paper.

- D. H. Lawrence, "Escape"

meta • noia
Noun - (me-ta-noi- ə\) :
A transformative change of heart

Transitions, *transformations, metamorphosis*—change. Sometimes we get stuck in the muck of our life and then, **WHAM!** We get blind-sided. Don't you know in order to provoke radical change we often need bigger, harder, attention-getting events than the subtleties of sweet quiet change that happen all the time, hidden from our eyes?

Ten years ago a cinematographer I knew named Mark Vicente showed up at my house. Hello **WHAM!** From that day onward neither my life *(nor me!)* would ever be the same. Mark introduced me to a little documentary he was making with **Will Arntz** about the science of spirituality then called, *Sacred Science. It wouldn't be exaggerating to say that that visit pulled me out of the ashes of a life in ruins.*

> **We delight in the beauty of the butterfly, but rarely admit the changes it has gone through to achieve that beauty.**
> - Author Unknown

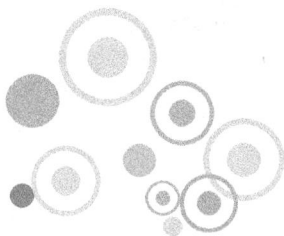

The movie we ended up making bore no resemblance to the little documentary script I read in my LA apartment that day *(the apartment I was about to be evicted from!)*. Instead it grew and grew, until three years later we ended up releasing the international hit hybrid documentary film, *What The Bleep Do We Know?!*

By making "The Bleep," this girl from The Valley who had never uttered the words *"quantum physics"* in her life was thrust into the New Age / New Thought spotlight. There I was, standing in front of hundreds of people in audiences all over the country, talking as if I knew something about the subject simply because I had read a few books, interviewed some people and made a movie about it!

A few weeks ago, **just for fun**, I went back and re-read some of the media interviews I was asked to give while the frenzy over "What the Bleep" was at its peak. ***Oh my! Did I really say that?*** Boy, was I the girl who knew it all! My life was perfect. **I was perfect.** I had everything figured out. And I was there to tell everybody else how to do it, just like me. *(Insert Ironic Laugh here.)*

A whole decade would slip by all warm and cozy in my infinite wisdom, lulled into a *false sense of security* knowing I had it all figured out. Asleep while I thought I was awake.

WHAM! Almost ten years after Mark's visit, my life is once again a shattered mess! *Fragments of my past perfection now lie strewn about like exploded shrapnel.* Funny how my soul's adventures seem to occur in decades—with every new decade bringing some huge shift. It's almost comforting, now, to know my pattern. This time it's almost as if I expected it—yearned for it. Why I couldn't just do it without the knife to my heart, I don't know. I guess I still need a push off the cliff to get me to really shift (stubborn much?)!

> **Any transition serious enough to alter your definition of self will require not just small adjustments in your way of living and thinking but a full-on metamorphosis.**
> -Martha Beck

But this time around I'm not afraid of the unknown that has arrived at my door. Oh, don't get me wrong, I cry. I dwell on the scary thoughts. But now I do it with a sort of detachment. It's as if I've split into two people. There's the "me" that is frightened and angry, and the "me" that knows it will all work out. *Don't you know, it always does!*

I am currently experiencing my own **metanoia**. Some word, huh? Carl Jung said that metanoia is a psychotic break (JEEZ – I don't want that!). But don't worry, this type of break is actually positive. Webster's calls it a "transformational change of heart," and ya know, that definition fits.

This **WHAM!** has led me to a self-healing and a pretty big reality check.

Now, I'm swimming around in this sea of the unknown, happy to finally admit, "I don't know shit." As Prickle from the kid's TV show *Gumby* used to say, *"I'm a nobody and I'm glad."* Contrary to what I thought ten years ago, I am nowhere near enlightened. And now that the self-constructed know-it-all walls of "me" are down, I realize I thrive in life's mystery.

The greatest realization I've had over the past few months is that I don't even know myself. For years I've been spouting the words of others— repeating them like a parrot, thinking that was what I was supposed to say and *be*. Now the question inside me is, now what? *I want to find me.* I want to know me. But to do that first I've got to exorcise the demons of the me that I am not.

> **Change and growth take place when a person has risked himself and dares to become involved with experimenting with his own life.**
> -Herbert Otto

The essays here are an **exploration of my mind** and an exorcism of the thoughts, feelings and beliefs of others *I've carried for far too long*.

I am filled with gratitude for the experiences of my life, and surprised I am grateful that they are neither perfect nor easy. Even as I wrote these essays—many filled with such hurt and anger—I felt peaceful. Just getting the words out of my head has been an amazing *release*. I feel a freedom in exposing my mind—the **good**, the **bad** and the *ugly*. *For I am all of those things and more.*

I am always **changing**—moving forwards then backwards. I am not what anyone has defined me to be, or even what I have defined myself to be. I just am one little soul experiencing life, stumbling through it moment-by-moment, realizing that finding joy is easy. **All I have to do is choose it.**

walk • of • shame

The longest walk of shame—*from the Eastside to Westside at 6 am*—LA streets as dirty as I felt. Even as the lawns became greener and the driveways l o n g e r I still couldn't drag myself up out of the gutter of my life.

How is it I have become trash thrown in the city street? Where is a good street cleaner when you need one? Oh, wait, that would be *me*. But I can't seem to do it—to wash the dirt from my soul. If I did I might see the message clearly drawn on the window: "Hear me. See me. I desire for you to know that you are worthy of love."

But I don't want to know that. *I must not.* I've kept the window filmed for so long, the dirt formed from memories of my past. To wash it away would be to wash myself away … the me that hangs on so tightly to *pity*, self-l o a t h i n g and rage. The dirt is my shield—my paltry defense against the pain I might feel if I actually let myself let go.

But the dirt is so thick at times it chips away of its own weight and I glimpse a letter, a word. I know what it says, even if I can't see it all. It's not that I don't know. It's that I'm afraid. It's not like I haven't tried. I just seem to fail at this one thing.

> " The resistance to the unpleasant situation is the root of suffering.
>
> - Ram Das

Love of self. **Love myself.** *Unconditional* love of self. It doesn't matter how many times or ways I write it, think it, say it— it's just e m p t y words I repeat hoping one day I might actually *mean it.*

At what point did I stop loving myself? *Did I ever even begin?* Why did it happen? Does it even matter? I've listened to every guru, every teacher—even that old lady on the street corner that LA morning so many years ago. *Love yourself* she muttered as she watched me s l i n k past her as she pushed her cart down the alley.

They all make it sound so simple.
Love yourself. *Forgive* yourself. I can't or won't. *Forget your past.* What am I without it? **Live in the moment.** I would, except these moments are filled with **doubt** and **pain** and **fear**. I'd rather live somewhere else thank you.

Be in the now. Yeah? *Well the NOW sucks!* Can't I live in the *future now* where it doesn't? If everything is happening simultaneously then how come I'm the one in this *now*? I'll happily trade with another me in another now. Fuck you NOW.

Now I have to forgive myself for being such a victim of my NOW. *I'll add that to my to do list.*

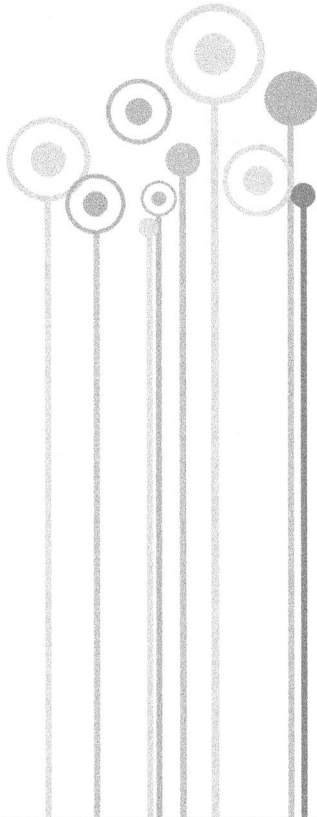

ʺ Self-love seems so often unrequited.
- Anthony Powell

ʺ I think knowing what you cannot do is more important than knowing what you can.
-Lucille Ball

know • me

I have been told I am not vulnerable enough. I have been called mean and horrible. **I have been called a tyrant.** I have been called sweet and l o v i n g and *kind*. How is it possible to be both, I wonder? *And yet, I see it's possible to be All.*

As I sit with you and talk with you and befriend you and marry you—as we share our **deepest** desires and **darkest** secrets—I know I am not *telling you anything*. As I smile and laugh at your jokes, I hide the **darkness** of my mind from you. I see behind the twinkle of your eyes that you, too, are hiding from me.

> **Knowing others is wisdom, knowing yourself is Enlightenment.**
> -Lao Tzu

What does it mean to be vulnerable?
I no longer know that word. I was vulnerable once. And, like a child burning their hand on a hot stove, I learned not to touch that heat again.

> **We are cups, constantly and quietly being filled. The trick is, knowing how to tip ourselves over and let the beautiful stuff out.**
> -Ray Bradbury

But now, after hiding for so long, I can't hide anymore. You want to know me—

then know me.

energy • vampire

You walk the streets by day and by night—no fear of darkness, no fear of the sun. You thrive on the light both inside and out, feeding until all is dark and empty.

You came toward me soft and slow, with all the nobleness of the lifetimes you had drained away. Your eyes pierced my wall, seeing my light—the light I myself could not see. Lost in my darkness I was pulled into your abyss, mistakenly thinking I saw your light. I did not yet know it was a light stolen from others.

You courted me and preyed on my sweetness. I became *addicted* to your tenderness, body and mind *hypnotized* by your caresses. *All of it carefully orchestrated to consume my light.* Leaving me empty and dark, pale and starving—filled now only with my own thirst.

I allowed you in and for a while found my light, blinding me with Bliss. *Was it real?* Did I actually experience joy? I hold onto the belief that I did. *Even as you were sucking my light away, I believed.*

What does one do when their life has been a lie? *How was it possible?* Each moment a life in itself. Now I get it—*multiple lives*—multiple moments strung together, connected by a single string that is me. Lost in a trance created by the taste of your blood.

Now, I have emerged from the darkness—starving, cold and weak. Amazed at the light that surrounds me, in awe of the love and light from others. But I fear that from our moments together I have emerged from our chrysalis an Energy Vampire, just like you. *Isn't that what a vampire does?* You suck all the light from me, and now I must go in search of my own victims because I no longer see how I can create my own.

> **Dare to reach out your hand into the darkness, to pull another hand into the light.**
> - Norman B. Rice

> **I slept with faith & found a corpse in my arms on awakening; I drank & danced all night with doubt & found her a virgin in the morning.**
> -Aleister Crowley

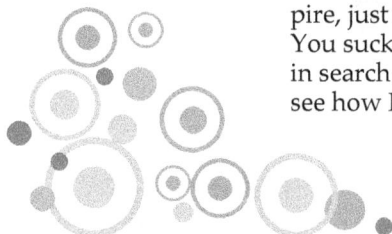

battle • cry

No matter what, I am still standing. I might cry and fight and grieve—but you cannot break my spirit. *It is invincible.*

In this life I have fallen many times—*fallen hard.* But I am a **phoenix**. I always come back, born anew—wiser and stronger and with gratitude for the fall.

Each hit seems harder and **meaner**, but it doesn't matter. *You will not break me.* I am stronger than you because I know I deserve to be *loved.* Your barbed words and burnished steel mean nothing. They break against the shield of my soul.

You can thrash about until you can't go on anymore ... exhausted by the battle from which you can never be free. *For you only fight yourself.*

I am free. I hear my soul crying out to me, *"You ARE LOVED!"* But you cannot hear the voice—mine or yours—buried under the relentless clang of your sword. But I can. Louder and louder as you hit harder and harder. You, mighty warrior, are no match for my heart and s o u l . Each stroke makes me stronger, don't you see? *You are attacking your own soul, thinking it is me.*

I am love—even as I fight the anger and grief. Forgiveness and futile attempts at reason are my skirmishes against you. But you can't see I fight you with love. You can't hear me under the sound of your battle cries as you strike again and again and again...

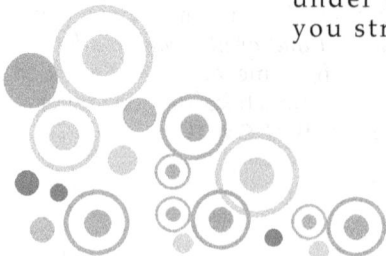

> ❝ A quarrel is quickly settled when deserted by one party; there is no battle unless there be two.
>
> - Lucius Annaeus Seneca

> ❝ It is better to conquer yourself than to win a thousand battles. Then the victory is yours.
>
> - Buddha

agree • ments

Y ou and I have an agreement: to serve each other's *addictions, needs* and *desires*. From the first word spoken we entered into this agreement. *If not, then you wouldn't be here, nor would I.* We would have simply moved on to the next person, waiting to see if they would agree.

We crave the rush. Even hunt for it daily, in every interaction—waiting for the agreement. It's like a drug cascading through our brains and bodies, like that first hit of ecstasy I took when I was 22. We are awash in the joy of finding another who will feed us for a time.

> **What we call reality is an agreement that people have arrived at to make life more livable**
>
> - Louise Nevelson

You know the feeling—like that first taste of coffee and puff of morning cigarette. Ahhhh. It will feel like forever in the beginning.

It doesn't even matter if the person on the other end actually is who I've dressed them up to be. *In a flash I've painted your face with my perfect perception of what I want you to be.* And for a while you unknowingly play along. You've painted me too.

> **Only that in you which is me can hear what I'm saying.**
>
> -Baba Ram Das

How decidedly unromantic to think of our relationships as agreements! Contracts entered into with a twinkle in our eyes. *But then the twinkle fades. We grow weary of playing the game.* We desire new rules and suddenly, like quicksand pulling us deeper into a pit, *that beautiful agreement is over.*

I hold on so tight! *How dare you try and escape it!* I smother it until there is no breath left—it dies and I keep its corpse in a little shrine within me, afraid that if I let it go *I might never find anyone else to agree again.*

But I do. I start the cycle all over again. *The agreement may change a bit.* I might have added an addendum from the lessons learned from my last failed contract. But at its core it's still the same. Isn't it?

All we are is an agreement between two people, lasting for a moment in time.

" We seldom find any person of good sense, except those who share our opinions.

-Francois De La Rochefoucauld

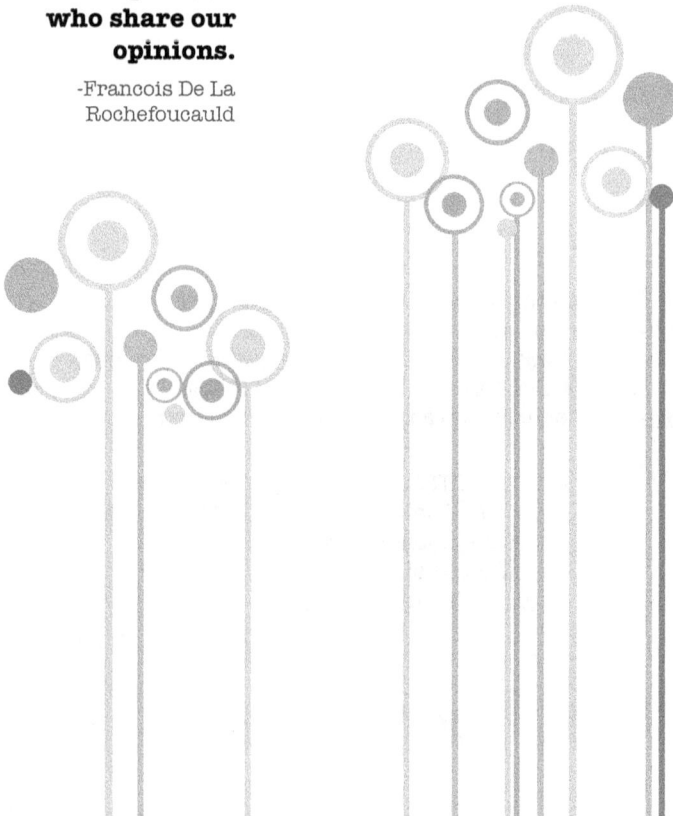

re • incarnation

Have you ever woken up and wondered who you were? *Where you were?* Everything seems familiar and you know everyone's name but your own?

I feel as though I've awakened into another life. Reincarnated into this new **Betsy Chasse** with fragments of childlike pictures strewn before me like a mism a t c h e d collage. Disjointed images make up my life—*the new or the old I cannot tell.*

I reach for a memory. Who was my first kiss? My first love? It seems odd that I can't remember these things … these **memories** we give such importance to. They seem to have meant nothing. Or m a y b e t h e y n e v e r h a p p e n e d ? *Why can't I recall?*

I must have lived them, right? *Everyone does.* But in which life? The images I do see before me I clutch close as if to confirm I did actually live before today. I look for the story of my life. *That flimsy piece of string that connects all these moments together.*

My memories feel so separate from me— like different lives, each a complete, distant story. *I go to sleep and wake up someone else.*

How long have I slept this time? When will I wake up?

Hunger for the drug that is normal life pulls me from my morning thoughts. It puts my feet onto the floor, accepting the story once again. Not today—tomorrow I'll wake up, I *promise*. Who knows who I'll be?

> **I know I am deathless. We have thus far exhausted trillions of winters and summers. There are trillions ahead, and trillions ahead of them.**
> - Walt Whitman

silver • ware

You take the spoons. I keep the forks. You take the fish. I keep the dog. *So easily we split the stuff we have acquired together!* But the blame? Apparently that's something we cannot, or will not, split. *It has to be either mine, or yours.*

Can't we share that too? Why can't it be like the spoons? *Wait!* There is no spoon. Was there ever an "us"? *Was there ever a you or a me?*

If **reality** is all in my mind and I create it, then I created a *you*, which is really a me creating a you to have an experience with.

Hmmm ... *I don't like that.* I'd rather just blame you. I'd rather swim in the muck of my own creation and continue the charade. The separateness of **me** and **you**—that is what I have created for safety's sake. *That is what I perpetuate.* Amazing isn't it—the cage we put ourselves in and then rail against? All so I can blame you and pretend it's not me that I despise.

> **No matter where you go or what you do, you live your entire life within the confines of your head.**
> -Terry Josephson

> **Be empty of worrying. Think of who created thought! Why do you stay in prison, When the door is so wide open?**
> - Rumi

forced • exile

I am living a life I did not chose or plan for. Of course, I must have wanted this experience, this feeling of exile from the life of my dreams. *Or else it wouldn't have happened.*

I am **lost** in the silence, unsure of what to do with my time. When you're here I crave peace. But it's your chaos I love. I have made it my life, and when you're away I miss you. *My days are spent planning around you.* You are my life, my soul running around the yard. In the quiet I try to make plans—but all I can do is sit in the yard wishing for your laughter.

I try sleeping-in like I did during those days of my youth. *But I can't.* I wake up missing your sweet smile, missing being pulled from slumber by your kicks and pokes. **"Wake up mommy, I want to play!"**

I miss waiting to see what wonders await you today, seeing the joy in your eyes. I want to share every moment with you. Kiss every bump and bruise and hold your hand along the way.

My phone calls to you cause me such pain—your little voice so distant. I want to reach out and hold you. Tell you it will all be okay, that I love you—a love unlike anything I've ever felt. *I'm so sorry for your hurt.* I'm sorry I let you down. I am sorry your dreams were shattered so young.

I promise you will have new ones. Don't give up on your dreams my sweet babies. I whisper these promises from afar, exiled to this place of solitude where I cannot kiss you goodnight.

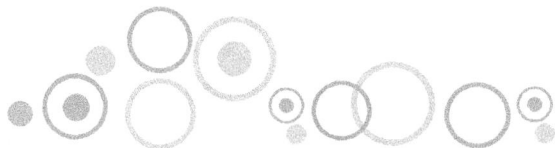

> **A rose can say "I love you," orchids can enthrall, but a weed bouquet in a chubby fist, yes, that says it all.**
>
> - Author Unknown

> **The day the child realizes that all adults are imperfect, he becomes an adolescent; the day he forgives them, he becomes an adult; the day he forgives himself, he becomes wise.**
>
> - Alden Nowlan

choices • are • mine

There is a moment each morning before we fully awaken when the world is not yet fully formed—when there is no **me**, no **you**.

Everything just is.

In this **moment** before awakening I can be anything I choose. **My soul is fulfilled.** My heart is warm with love. The hurt of yesterday is past—until I put my feet on the floor. *So I keep them tucked away under the blankets.*

I linger between worlds, basking in the glow of being—being you, being me, being everything *all at once.* Understanding, forgiving, accepting, finding grace and gratitude knowing all is good. N o w — I h a v e t o d a y .

I choose joy.
I choose love.
I choose peace.

And though they will be challenged countless times today, I find comfort in knowing that the choice is mine. **I feel the power of choice** ... and only then place my feet upon the floor.

> **When love and hate are both absent everything becomes clear and undisguised.**
> - Osho

> **Each day is a new canvas to paint upon. Make sure your picture is full of life and happiness, and at the end of the day you don't look at it and wish you had painted something different.**
> - Unknown

it • burns

I wonder if you'll still be sweet when I'm through with you? I was sweet once too— before I drank from the cup of love. *Then I choked on the grit at the bottom of my glass.*

Poison cascades through my system. At first it's a *warm burn*—the kind that makes you melt with desire. But soon the burn turns hot, the sweetness turns sour! So hot, so sour it suffocates. I am unable even to scream.

How does it happen that love hurts so much? **No one ever told me about the pain.** I only heard sweet whispers—even as my flesh began to melt away.

Next time I will be ready.

Next time?

I promise not to love you. And you should not love me. *Let's just pretend for a while.* Being leery of the heat, lest we get **burned**.

> **I see when men love women. They give them but a little of their lives. But women when they love give everything.**
>
> - Oscar Wilde

> **Love can sometimes be magic. But magic can sometimes... just be an illusion.**
>
> - Javan

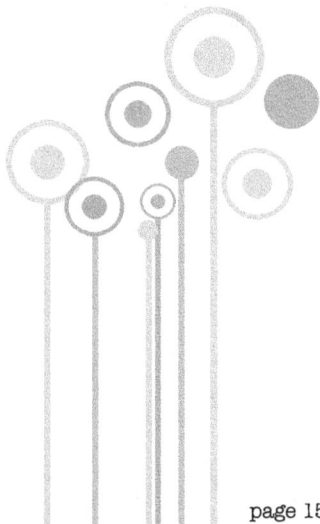

the • first • kiss

It was a first **kiss** like no other. It wasn't the same as my first first kiss—*sweet with nervous anticipation*. It wasn't the first kiss of the father of my children—layered with the **expectation** of promises that won't be kept. That kiss started a *fire* that burned out a long time ago. But the embers lay **smoldering**, waiting to be lit again.

After being caged for so long—after her children are born and the love she once held so gently has **shattered** in her hands—*a woman dreams of this first kiss*. Fighting with the fear of being old and forgotten and unlovely, it lives in her head—*the only safe place this kiss might dwell*.

But then it comes. It's *unexpected*. Not from the one she imagined. That makes it oh so much sweeter, doesn't it?

This *kiss* holds no promises to be broken. This kiss won't burn me anytime soon. *This kiss has no planned future.* It's the kiss of **freedom**, soft and sweet, penetrating with just enough force to push me off the ledge to *spread my wings once more.*

> **Something opens our wings. Something makes boredom and hurt disappear. Someone fills the cup in front of us: We taste only sacredness.**
> - Rumi

> **Lips that taste of tears, they say, are the best for kissing.**
> - Dorothy Parker

hera

You can have my body. I'll sell you my wisdom for a *drop of love*. I don't even care if it's **real**. Just a good show will do. I don't need a lot. Just enough to quench my thirst.

I'll teach you the ways of a woman. Not just any woman—but the wife you dream of. *I'll teach you what she will desire.* More than once I've bled my soul to the goddess of hearth and home. **I know the territory.**

It will not be me at the altar with you. There isn't any blood left. Hera has had her fill of me. And, dare I say, me of her.

I was an early devotee. Had it all planned out—the picture perfectly constructed in my head from the fairy tales of youth ... wife, husband, kids and the dog. *Sigh.*

Then I woke up! Realized I'd been lied to! Realized I'd been held captive all this time, asleep with the promise of love. Wandering through life—**desperate** for the dream to visit again so I could kneel at her alter and *pour out more blood.*

But now, as I lie withered at her feet, I know the price.

I will teach you, my love, the lessons that cost me my soul. *The lessons you need to snare that perfect bride.*

First Lesson: believe the lie.

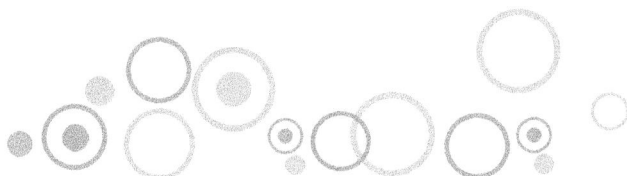

> **Deceiving others. That is what the world calls a romance.**
> - Oscar Wilde

> **Love: A temporary insanity curable by marriage.**
> - Ambrose Bierce

warnings

I do not hate you. **I pity you.** I feel sad in knowing your end. *I tried to warn you*—but it was too late. You'd already drunk from the goblet of "**love**."

How many times have we all been warned of our choices?
How many times have we not heeded wise words from those who have trod the path before us? *But we know better, don't we?* We're wiser than those who came before us. Even as we read the writing on the wall, we ignore it. We are special, *different,* **better**.

> **History is a vast early warning system.**
> - Norman Cousins

Oh Bliss – blinding us from what we should see. Or what we refuse to see. Those little signs like stains in an old rug keep popping up. And we scrub harder as we chant **"not me"**.

And then it's too late.

> **I may do some good before I am dead— be a sort of success as a frightful example of what not to do; and so illustrate a moral story.**
> - Thomas Hardy

Suddenly you realize you ARE just another stain. Now you see them all, don't you? And you realize the danger signs were everywhere. Those stains cover every inch of your world. How is it possible you missed them? **I know, I missed them too.**

Don't feel bad. You're not alone. We understand—those who came before you. Even though you laughed at us, we're here to catch you when you, too, fall from grace.

I know you don't hear me now. But you will.

composting

After the crash—after we have taken in the carnage, we go forward. It's all we can do. *And each time it gets easier.*

Even as I sit with my grief, I know it will not last forever. *That is the gift of wisdom.* I can already see the sprouts of newness poking up from the dirt. **Pushing their way out of the soil—rotting as it may be.** a

Decomposing fruit and yesterday's news smelling of tiredness. I consider it with gratitude. It's my compost and I have no regrets. I watch it turn from rot to black gold, *excitedly waiting to see what will rise to the surface.*

Sometimes little sprouts, nourished by lessons learned, begin to grow. Sometimes the flower is the same—the message of the soul gone unheeded.

But this time I have heard.
I emerge from this soil brighter, refreshed, petals soft, renewed—and now, with a stronger stem.

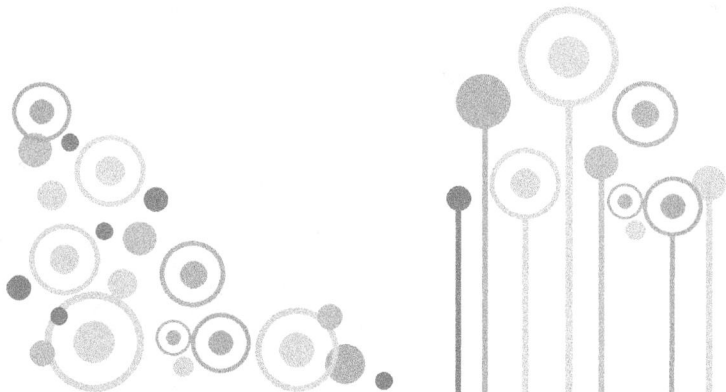

> **So as long as a person is capable of self-renewal, they are a living being.**
> - Henri Frederic Amiel

> **The ground's generosity takes in our compost and grows beauty! Try to be more like the ground.**
> - Rumi

believe • in • magic

I still believe in magic. I believe in faeries, brownies and pixies—well maybe not the three-inch kind. But as I have aged, so have they—their tricks and pranks taking on a more *sinister* tone.

There are definitely witches—I've been called one often enough *(and I don't think they were thinking of Glinda)*. There are dark lords and white wizards abounding. All that has been created is—
Magic.

I know, some call it s c i e n c e. Some call it **God**. But life, to me, is magic.

> **A world in which elves exist and magic works offers greater opportunities to digress and explore.**
> - Terry Brooks

> **If you see the magic in a fairy tale, you can face the future.**
> - Danielle Steele

Even as my heart lies bleeding, barely pumping, jettisoned to the side of the road, I still believe in **magic**. I am that 5 year-old girl with the spider hidden in my curtains, waiting for it to spell its name. *I sobbed as my mother removed the gigantic arachnid.* **Opportunity lost!**

The little girl is still playing princess, waiting patiently *(sort of)* for her prince. Only now I see the **princes** and **knights**—all the white wizards and dark lords—*as reflections of me.* Pieces of my soul appearing in a prism (prison?) of my own creation. Little bits of light, reflecting my own disguise.

Often, I don't like what I see. *Who does?* But even as I'm forced to grow and change *(Oh my!)* I still believe in magic.

whispers • of • the • soul

So ... I'm sitting here staring at my favorite picture of you ... looking into those incredible soul-piercing eyes, feeling immense **gratitude**. Adoring, appreciating your sweet spirit for being here when I needed you.

Don't worry—no fantasies of a future. Just, grateful for the *now*.

Your t o u c h is tender and kind, your kiss *soft and loving*. Oh, how I needed to be reminded how it could be! Your lips whisper to me. I wonder, do you even know what they say?

> **Nothing can cure the soul but the senses, just as nothing can cure the senses but the soul.**
>
> - Oscar Wilde

It doesn't matter. Even if you aren't saying anything, **my soul is**. Maybe it's using your lips because that's the only way I'll hear. *Through the kiss of another comes healing* because I won't accept it any other way.

Stubborn me. Thank God *my soul* hasn't given up on me yet! It stops at nothing, using every means possible to make me hear that I am ... dare I say it? I am worthy of love.

> **For it was not into my ear you whispered, but into my heart. It was not my lips you kissed, but my soul.**
>
> - Judy Garland

Amazing this voice we ignore so often. So many signs! *If only I would hear*. If only I would **believe**. Don't stop my old friend. I will hear you—I do now even though I will forget tomorrow. *Now I hear you*. Someday I will believe for good.

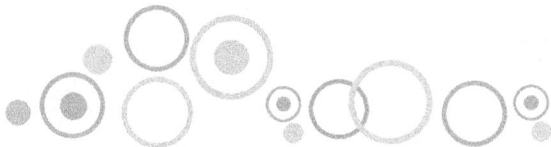

love • in • the • aftermath

I do love falling in love—even as I see it's not real and not what I *thought* love should be. I don't seem to mind. **Not now.** After all the betrayals given and received, this love is oddly refreshing and new.

I look at you **across the table** and it's what I don't think about that *excites me*. I really don't **care** what you do for a living. I don't care if you like your parents. There will be no comingled bank accounts, shared property or children from **this exchange.**

I do not **hang my future** on your shoulders, nor my past. With you I am simply *now*, bathed in the green of your eyes. *They, too, have no plans for me.* Well ... maybe a few ...

> **Heaven would indeed be heaven if lovers were there permitted as much enjoyment as they had experienced on earth.**
> - Giovanni Boccaccio

Pure and **sweet** and **naughty**, ours is a relationship built solely on **PLEASURE.** We explore the word, *free from fears of entrapment*, being who we want to be without reflection. **No rings.** No promises. You are not my father. I am not your mother and this is not our wedding night.

> **Lovers don't finally meet somewhere. They're in each other all along.**
> - Rumi

We are simply two souls who **long to feel loved.** Not the love of youth. *Thank God!* This love has no dreams to uphold.

One day we won't be lovers anymore. But I will always remember you as my **first love in the aftermath.**

demons

Be careful what you **wish** for. That's what the fairytales say. Even if you don't realize you're wishing, *be wary of those thoughts you focus on for they just might come true.*

But maybe they should come true, those fears we keep hidden. Manifest that we might *face* them, stand and show them who is in charge. *We summon them, after all.*

I've always had a fear of flying. **Yet I get on that airplane every time.** But my darkest fear—the one I dare not say aloud even to myself—*dare I bring it to full light?*

Being abandoned and alone.

There, I said it. *I've written it.* Now you know my greatest fear and what I am finally facing.

Funny thing is, I'm so grateful for experiencing it. Now, out of the shadows, I see it clearly. *Standing tall, I look at it dead-on.*

It's so much smaller than when it was a thought monster, living in my head. Its teeth are less green. Its eyes not nearly so red and beady. *Oh, the little monsters we conjure as children turn so much meaner as we age!*

Yet here I am, standing tall and laughing as my greatest demon is turning and running away. **I am still here.**

> **I'm not this dark, twisted person. Yes, I have my demons and this is my way of exorcising them. It gets them out—and better out than in.**
> - Naomi Watts

> **It is better to reenter hell and become an angel, than to remain in heaven and become a demon.**
> - Victor Hugo

belief

An acceptance that something exists or is true, especially one without proof.

That's an awfully small word to be so powerful. Yet from the moment we are born it's what makes us move. *It's what makes everything move.*

Everything is meaningless—even life—until we assign it meaning and *believe* in that meaning. When I was a baby my every cry had meaning behind it, even if I didn't consciously know it at the time *(or even know that I was an I trying to express meaning).* Did my mother get my messages? Or did she just believe she did, making up her own meanings to match my infant sounds? Or did she read all the childcare books and believe what the experts wrote?

Isn't that what we all do all the time? *Make up our own beliefs,* or borrow them from somebody else?

Today *I'm filled with beliefs* I've made up, been educated to b e l i e v e or borrowed from the people I have collected throughout my life. And all these thousands of little beliefs run my life. They determine my choices, my successes and my failures. *Every* relationship, *every* encounter, *every* decision is t a i n t e d with beliefs I'm carrying around from God knows where.

One belief I have carried for too long is that I am unworthy of love. *(Whose love?)* Another is I believe I'm not smart enough *(For whom?).* I believe that I am ugly and short *(in whose eyes?).* How can I prove any of these beliefs are my own?

Only through my attachment to them.

> **The mark of your ignorance is the depth of your belief in injustice and tragedy. What the caterpillar calls the end of the world, the Master calls the butterfly.**
> - Richard Bach

> **Man is made by his belief. As he believes, so he is.**
> - Johann Wolfgang von Goethe

Damn! This shit is heavy and I just don't want to carry it anymore.

It's like moving after 20 years in the same location and looking in the basement. *Where the hell did all that stuff come from?!*

I think I'll take back those beliefs.

Exchange them for something lighter, more airy and uplifting. *More me.*

I am loveable, if for no one else but myself. I am capable and smart and, ya know what? I am damn beautiful too!

Ahhh. I feel lighter already.

> **Beliefs have the power to create and the power to destroy. Human beings have the awesome ability to take any experience of their lives and create a meaning that disempowers them or one that can literally save their lives.**
>
> - Tony Robbins

"Tell me one last thing," said Harry. *"Is this real?* Or has this been happening inside my head?"

**"Of course
it has been happening
inside your head, Harry -
but why on earth should
that mean it is not real?"**

- J.K. Rowling, Harry Potter and the Deathly Hallows

Special Thanks to:
Cate Montana, Renee Slade, Ri Stewart, Melissa Henderson,
Gabrielle Sagona, Anna West, David James Kuhr,
my family—my mom, my sister and brothers—
and to all my friends who have shown me the true
meaning of love and friendship. I am forever grateful to you all.

L isted in Variety's top 50 Independent Producers of 2004, Betsy Chasse has helped produce over 30 feature films, and runs her own production and distribution company, Intention Media, which has released multiple films on DVD or in theaters including the Sundance Award winning documentary FUEL, the award winning *"Quantum Activist"* and most recently *"2012 Time For Change"* and the newest film from Bleep co-creator Will Arntz *"Ghetto Physics"*.

Chasse was the co-creator and is credited with co-writing, co-directing and producing, What The Bleep Do We Know?! "BLEEP" is the 5th highest grossing documentary in U.S history and still enjoys a strong presence on DVD.

In 2005 Chasse co-authored the book *What The Bleep Do We Know?! Discovering the endless possibilities for altering your everyday reality,* now in its fifth printing.

In 2007 she produced the documentary Pregnant in America. Pregnant In America was released in 2008 by Intention Media and was screened nationally and endorsed by leading birth experts such as Lamaze International and Midwife Association of America.

She is currently completing a new screenplay *"Killing Buddha"* which is loosely based on her journey of making *"BLEEP"*.

Chasse is a highly sought after speaker on such subjects as spirituality, the blending of science and spirituality, and marketing to the cultural creative demographic.

Chasse most enjoys organic gardening and spending time with her two children Elorathea and Maximus.